BERLIN
THE CITY AT A GLANCE

W9-CMI-503

Reichstag
Parliament moved into Foster + Partners'
remodelled building in 1999, and the spiral
stairs in its glass dome enchant visitors.
Platz der Republik 1, T 2273 2152

Brandenburg Gate
Alternately a symbol of victory, separation
and reunification, Carl Gotthard Langhans'
1791 Greek Revival arch is an icon of Berlin.
Pariser Platz

Holocaust Memorial
One of several highly significant monuments
that confront Germany's turbulent past.
See p034

Internationales Handelszentrum
The GDR made this anything-you-can-do
modernist statement in 1978, a trade centre
designed by Erhardt Gisske and financed
by the Japanese. Its 96m still pack a punch.
Friedrichstrasse 95

Berliner Dom
Looming handsomely over Museum Island,
this outsized historicist church, completed in
1905, has a glorious dome and great views.
Lustgarten, T 2026 9136

Fernsehturm
GDR leaders were dismayed to realise that
the sun's reflection off their 1969 'ball on a
spike' TV Tower appeared as a giant crucifix.
See p015

Rotes Rathaus
Completed in 1869 in neo-Renaissance style,
the red-brick City Hall has a 74m clocktower.
It's home to mayor Klaus Wowereit, who gave
Berlin its 'poor but sexy' tag a decade ago.
Rathausstrasse 15

INTRODUCTION
THE CHANGING FACE OF THE URBAN SCENE

Berlin is now firmly established as one of the world's great cultural capitals. What it lacks in financial clout, when compared with other big German cities such as Frankfurt or Munich, it compensates for with energy, creative buzz and an embracing of ideas. Its art fairs and exhibitions, including the Biennale and ABC Art Berlin Contemporary, draw global attention, and Fashion Week is a key fixture in the style arena. In 2017, it will finally get a major airport suited to its status as one of the most-visited cities in Europe. But the sleek Brandenburg International has already been delayed three times, so locals will only believe it when they see it.

It is not unusual for a casual visitor to the city to end up as a permanent resident, and new Berliners abound, opening galleries, studios and shops in still-plentiful underused urban spaces. As a result of this influx, the cheap rents have started to climb, pushing the culture crowd into one upcoming area after another.

Famously, this is a city that never sleeps. During the days of the Weimar Republic, the capital gained a reputation as a hedonistic party town, and the label still applies today. From underground events to hardcore techno clubs, the nightlife is as diverse as the city. It may have its edgy moments, but Berlin is comparatively safe. It has a well-run municipal infrastructure, and even after burning the candle at both ends, you are never far from the familiar warmth of a custard-coloured taxi to whisk you home.

ESSENTIAL INFO
FACTS, FIGURES AND USEFUL ADDRESSES

TOURIST OFFICE
Berlin Tourist Information
Pariser Platz
T 250 025
www.visitberlin.de

TRANSPORT
Airport transfer from Tegel to Mitte
JetExpressBus TXL
www.bvg.de
Buses depart regularly between 6am and
11pm. The journey takes 30 to 40 minutes
S-Bahn/U-Bahn
Trains run from 4am to 1am, Sunday to
Thursday; 24 hours, Fridays and Saturdays
Taxis
Funk Taxi Berlin
T 261 026
Cabs can also be hailed on the street
Travel card
A 72-hour WelcomeCard costs €25.50 and
includes discounts to many attractions
www.visitberlin.de

EMERGENCY SERVICES
Ambulance/Fire
T 112
Police
T 110
24-hour pharmacy
Apotheke Berlin Hauptbahnhof
T 2061 4190

EMBASSIES
British Embassy
Wilhelmstrasse 70
T 204 570
www.gov.uk/government/world/germany
US Embassy
Clayallee 170
T 8305 1200
germany.usembassy.gov

POSTAL SERVICES
Post office
Königstrasse 27-28
T 018 023 333
www.deutschepost.de
Shipping
UPS
T 018 0588 2663
www.ups.com

BOOKS
Berlin by Freunde von Freunden (Distanz)
Goodbye to Berlin
by Christopher Isherwood (Vintage)

WEBSITES
Architecture
www.german-architects.com
Art/Design
www.artnews.org
Newspaper
www.spiegel.de/international

EVENTS
Berlin Biennale
www.berlinbiennale.de
Berlin Design Week
www.berlin-design-week.com
Berlin Fashion Week
www.fashion-week-berlin.com

COST OF LIVING
Taxi from Tegel Airport to Mitte
€27
Cappuccino
€2.50
Packet of cigarettes
€5
Daily newspaper
€0.70
Bottle of champagne
€70

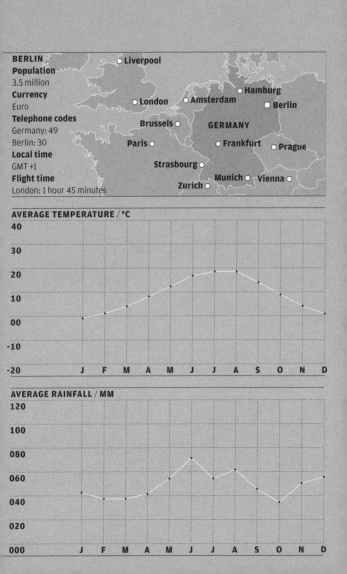

BERLIN
Population
3.5 million
Currency
Euro
Telephone codes
Germany: 49
Berlin: 30
Local time
GMT +1
Flight time
London: 1 hour 45 minutes

Liverpool
London
Amsterdam
Hamburg
Berlin
Brussels
GERMANY
Paris
Frankfurt
Prague
Strasbourg
Munich
Vienna
Zurich

AVERAGE TEMPERATURE / ℃

40											
30											
20											
10											
00											
-10											
-20	J	F	M	A	M	J	J	A	S	O	N	D

AVERAGE RAINFALL / MM

120											
100											
080											
060											
040											
020											
000	J	F	M	A	M	J	J	A	S	O	N	D

NEIGHBOURHOODS
THE AREAS YOU NEED TO KNOW AND WHY

To help you navigate the city, we've chosen the most interesting districts (see below and the map inside the back cover) and colour-coded our featured venues, according to their location; those venues that are outside these areas are not coloured.

TIERGARTEN

Past the Brandenburg Gate, Tiergarten is the location of the Reichstag (see p064) and the Haus der Kulturen der Welt (see p066), as well as modernist architectural gems by Oscar Niemeyer and Alvar Aalto in Hansaviertel. To the south, art galleries, such as Blain|Southern (Potsdamer Strasse 77-87, T 644 931 510), are commonplace.

SCHEUNENVIERTEL

Although it's touristy on the surface, Scheunenviertel's backstreets are packed with distinct boutiques, such as Lunettes Selection (see p076) and Apartment (see p084). In this area you'll find furniture and clothes by local designers, and big-label German stores like Hugo Boss and Adidas.

KREUZBERG

Once the hangout of left-wing punks and anarchists, Kreuzberg has transformed radically since reunification, but the place has kept its healthy cultural mix. During summer, it's a happy place to eat, chill out and socialise. A more sobering experience is the Jewish Museum (see p064).

FRIEDRICHSHAIN

First impressions tend to be of six-lane thoroughfares lined with epic communist-era architecture, and old stretches of the Wall covered in street art. But dive off into the side roads around Boxhagener Platz and you'll discover many cafés, bars, retro furniture shops and restaurants.

CHARLOTTENBURG

There's no question that Charlottenburg is a little duller for its gentrification, but Kurfürstendamm, the major shopping drag, is well worth a look, and this 'hood is where to stay for affordable luxury – at Hotel-Pension Dittberner (see p030), for example. Don't miss the Olympiastadion (see p089), built for the 1936 Games.

MITTE

After the Wall came down, the historic city centre was the first district to be smartened up. Today it is a dense mix of refurbished 18th- and 19th-century apartments, GDR *Plattenbauten* (prefabs) and new-builds. Modern architecture has sprung up in the derelict, war-torn gaps.

PRENZLAUER BERG

Many of the 19th-century houses in this once decaying working-class district have been spruced up and are now occupied by arty young families. The scene centres around Knaackstrasse and Kollwitzplatz. Lazy Sunday breakfasts are de rigueur, if the kids don't drive you to distraction.

SCHÖNEBERG

The verdant boroughs of former West Berlin are home to grand old hotels and a cluster of contemporary art galleries, most of which are hidden in courtyards along Potsdamer Strasse. From here, it's only a 20-minute drive to the lake-front beaches of the Wannsee (see p100).

LANDMARKS

THE SHAPE OF THE CITY SKYLINE

The landmark most visitors want to see is the one that no longer exists: the Berlin Wall. Forget the touristy mock-up of the former Checkpoint Charlie on Friedrichstrasse, and instead head for the more poignant Berlin Wall Memorial along the southern side of Bernauer Strasse (www.berliner-mauer-gedenkstaette.de).

Just as the traces left by the Wall are increasingly hard to find, so are differences between 'East' and 'West' as the city expands into the gaps left by history. The stretch of New Internationalist and Stalinist architecture from Alexanderplatz down Karl-Marx-Allee is very 'East', but you will struggle to find any communist drabness in the renovated area it leads to around Oberbaum City (overleaf) and the cafés on Mainzer Strasse in Friedrichshain.

Despite having functioned as two cities for 41 years, Berlin is well signposted and has an efficient transport system. The only headache is the doubling up of buildings, such as opera houses Deutsche Oper in the West (Bismarckstrasse 35, T 343 8401) and Staatsoper – under renovation until 2015 – to the East (Unter den Linden 7, T 2035 4555), and conference centres ICC (see p012) and BCC (Alexanderstrasse 11, T 2380 6750). Confusion over the two mainline stations, Ostbahnhof and Bahnhof Zoologischer Garten, located in the East and West, was resolved with the 2006 opening of Meinhard von Gerkan's central Hauptbahnhof (Europaplatz). *For full addresses, see Resources.*

Narva-Turm
The brick building that housed the Narva light-bulb factory and test laboratory east of Warschauer Strasse was redeveloped into offices in 2000 as part of the revamp of the Oberbaum City area. A large glass cube was added to the top, which, when lit up at night, is a 63m-high beacon to those heading out for a night's partying in Friedrichshain or Kreuzberg.
Rotherstrasse 8-26

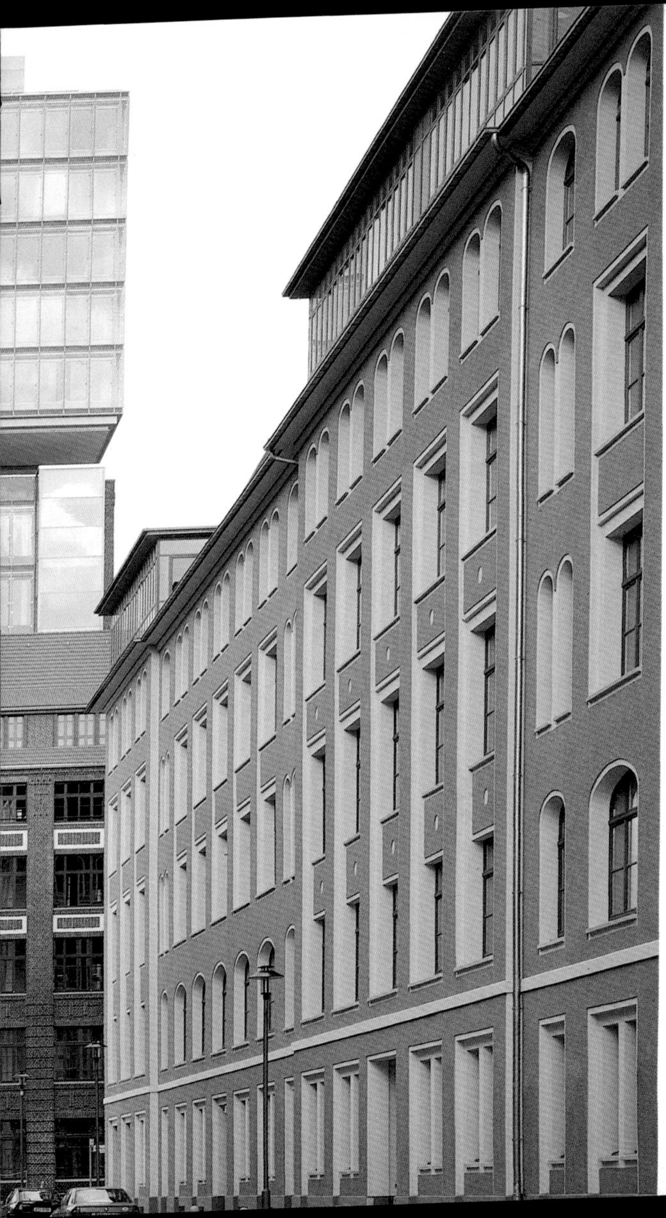

ICC

A great aluminium-clad monument to
the era when the car was king in the eyes
of town planners, this 1979 conference
hall, designed by Ralf Schüler and Ursulina
Schüler-Witte, featured an eight-lane
underground entrance that could process
650 vehicles in half an hour. It was state of
the art when it opened, due to electronic
information boards, 80 halls that can hold
14,500 people, and automated seating

that folds up to the ceiling to convert
Hall 2 into a concert venue. Once one of
the largest, most expensive buildings in
Germany, it had become something of a
dinosaur, overshadowed by multipurpose
event spaces such as O2 World (T 206 070
8826), and it closed in 2014 to undergo
a three-year, multimillion-euro revamp.
*Neue Kantstrasse/Ecke Messedamm,
www.icc-berlin.de*

GSW Headquarters

This update of a 1950s Kreuzberg high-rise, which has gentle curves and an ingenious chromatic facade of metal scales, placed local architects Sauerbruch Hutton on the map in 1999. The GSW HQ's west-facing double-skinned exterior is covered with blinds in white and shades of red, orange and pink, all of which open and close independently, regulating the building's heat and light levels and making for a stunning 22-storey piece of abstract art. The structure is best appreciated – in the glow of the evening sun – from the lounge of panoramic bar Solar (T 163 765 2700) on nearby Stresemannstrasse. A couple of blocks away is Mossehaus (Schützenstrasse 18-25). Its streamlined expressionist facade was added in 1922 after damage in WWI and was designed by Erich Mendelsohn. *Charlottenstrasse 4*

Kaiser-Wilhelm-Gedächtnis-Kirche

This large, originally unremarkable church, designed by Franz Heinrich Schwechten in 1895, was severely bomb-damaged during WWII. In the 1950s, debate raged about whether to tear it down or rebuild it. The eventual decision, a pioneering one, was to have Berlin's great functionalist architect Egon Eiermann adapt the ruined torso of the tower into a memorial chapel, and build a new church and belltower to go with it. Above the altar floats a huge golden statue of Christ with arms outstretched, by Munich artist Karl Hemmeter, while Gabriel Loire's stunning deep-blue honeycomb windows, flecked with red and gold, help to create a suitably reflective atmosphere in one of the most famous architectural monuments to the futility of war.
Breitscheidplatz, T 218 5023,
www.gedaechtniskirche-berlin.de

Fernsehturm

Berlin's tallest building, a bold 368m spike with a ball in the middle, was conceived by an architects' collective. Based on a 1960s concept by Hermann Henselmann and Jörg Streitparth, the TV Tower is one of the highlights of the New International architecture around the Alexanderplatz area, much of which has now, sadly, been obscured, 'modernised' or pulled down by unappreciative developers. The 1969 Fernsehturm, at least, has remained, and this former symbol of the German Democratic Republic has now become a signature structure of the unified city. The once-rather-queasy express lift has been replaced, so – if you can bear the queues – take the 40-second ride 207m up to the rotating Sphere restaurant (T 247 575 875) to drink in the views across Berlin. *Panoramastrasse 1a, www.tv-turm.de*

HOTELS

WHERE TO STAY AND WHICH ROOMS TO BOOK

Berlin is packed with hotels, but only in the late noughties did the dynamic east begin to get the properties it deserved (opposite). Cool boutique hotels have also popped up around Mitte, including Weinmeister (see p025) and Casa Camper (see p029), and the hip factor has spread west thanks to 25hours Hotel Bikini (see p024).

Prices are reasonable for a capital, and even the new hotels are more about affordable style than five-star perks. For slick service, look to the Regent (Charlottenstrasse 49, T 20 338) and Sofitel Kurfürstendamm (Augsburger Strasse 41, T 800 9990). If you are visiting during the Film Festival, a Potsdamer Platz address is a must; try the Grand Hyatt (Marlene-Dietrich-Platz 2, T 2553 1234).

Otherwise, head over to Tiergarten for Das Stue (see p020) or, nearby, the 2012 Waldorf Astoria (Hardenbergstrasse 28, T 814 0000), within a Christoph Mäckler-designed skyscraper. A good bet for Fashion Week is the stylish Lux 11 (Rosa-Luxemburg-Strasse 9-13, T 936 2800), while Gorki Apartments (see p018), Hotel de Rome (see p026) and the SEHW-designed Cosmo (Spittelmarkt 13, T 5858 2222) remain fine choices. The Karl Lagerfeld-decorated Schlosshotel im Grunewald (Brahmsstrasse 10, T 895 840), set in a 1912 mansion, is OTT in all the right ways. The most unique stay, however, is the sleek Modern Boat (Gustav-Holzmann-Strasse 10, T 0176 6411 5016) in Rummelsburger See on the Spree.

For full addresses and room rates, see Resources.

Michelberger Hotel

If the Michelberger, a quirky flashpacker-style hotel that opened in 2009, feels like the backdrop to an arthouse film, that's because set designer Sibylle Oellerich and actress Anja Knauer helped to dream up the interiors. The ground floor, which comprises a library, a bar and a doughnut-shaped reception area, is a stylish jumble of concrete and wooden floors, cuckoo clocks, mismatching fleamarket chairs, low couches and hanging lamps made from recycled hardcover books. Check into the Loft (above) or one of the four luxury rooms, such as The Chalet, a humorous Alpine-style attic with a ceiling of raw wood planks and a red-tiled shower room; or The Golden One, an opulent hideaway where every surface glitters. *Warschauer Strasse 39/40, T 2977 8590, www.michelbergerhotel.com*

Gorki Apartments

Each of the 34 options in this late 19th-century *Altbau* are unique. The work of architects Kim Wang and Sandra Pauquet, the apartments (H Schuhmacher, above) are decked in bespoke colour schemes, wallpapers and a mix of contemporary and vintage furniture, from Egon Eiermann desks to Knoll chairs or a fleamarket lamp. There are fitted kitchens, bathrooms feature subtle frescoes, glazed brick tiles and Dr Bronner organic products, while the soft furnishings are by local label Odeeh. The two top-floor penthouses (180 sq m and 200 sq m) are ideal for groups. A basement room is being repurposed as gallery space for emerging artists. Busy Rosenthaler Platz is just round the corner, or hire a Pelago bike to explore further.
Weinbergsweg 25, T 4849 6480,
www.gorkiapartments.de

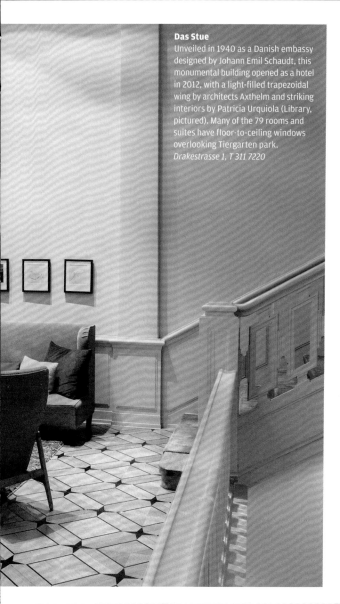

Das Stue
Unveiled in 1940 as a Danish embassy designed by Johann Emil Schaudt, this monumental building opened as a hotel in 2012, with a light-filled trapezoidal wing by architects Axthelm and striking interiors by Patricia Urquiola (Library, pictured). Many of the 79 rooms and suites have floor-to-ceiling windows overlooking Tiergarten park.
Drakestrasse 1, T 311 7220

Mani

This 63-room boutique hotel opened in 2012 a few blocks from its big sister, the Amano (T 809 4150), which has been an established stomping ground for Mitte's nightlife gentry since 2009. Mani is smaller, flashier and more sumptuous. Clusters of bamboo and tawny-hued distressed leather reflect off metal and black glass in a lobby replete with a library and photography by Oliver Rath. Rooms are simply divided into two categories, single and double; the latter, including Room 208 (above), are the more spacious. The interiors were designed by local firm Ester Bruzkus Architekten, also responsible for Tim Raue (see p038). The Israeli-French restaurant (opposite; T 530 280 8255), also called Mani, is likely to be the only spot in town where your foie gras burger includes quince, tahini and black truffle.
Torstrasse 136, T 5302 8080, www.hotel-mani.com

25hours Hotel Bikini

Crafted by Werner Aisslinger, who livened up the concrete with showy furnishings and playful touches, Bikini is located next to the zoo in a 1950s tower block by Paul Schwebes and Hans Schoszberger. On the third floor, a huge loft-like reception area (above) houses a bakery, a magazine and book kiosk, a 'Working Lab' office space and chillout areas enhanced by fur-lined hammocks, a Vitra swing sofa and a DJ corner. Down darkened corridors, the 149 rooms have illuminated numbers; inside it's all pine, raw surfaces and drawings on walls. Jungle Rooms look into the elephant and ape enclosures and Urban Rooms towards the city. On the upper floors are a sauna, a bar and a rooftop restaurant, Neni, serving East Mediterranean cuisine. *Budapester Strasse 40, T 120 2210, www.25hours-hotels.com*

The Weinmeister

The epicentre of Berlin-Mitte chic, The Weinmeister, which opened in 2010, is the consummate style-conscious introduction to the city. Adorning its walls are portraits of the many artists, actors and creatives who frequent the hotel. The British electro-pop band Hurts have their own room, the Hurts Chamber (above), which includes the duo's choice of books, CDs and DVDs alongside an oversized bed and an iMac (there's one in each of the 84 rooms). The graffiti-splattered entrance by Rene Turrek and stairwell mural by street-art collective Paint Club pay tribute to Berlin's reputation as a bohemian playground. The Schwarz Bar is named after German actress Jessica, also a regular here, but the rooftop terrace is the place to head for drinks in summer. *Weinmeisterstrasse 2, T 755 6670, www.the-weinmeister.com*

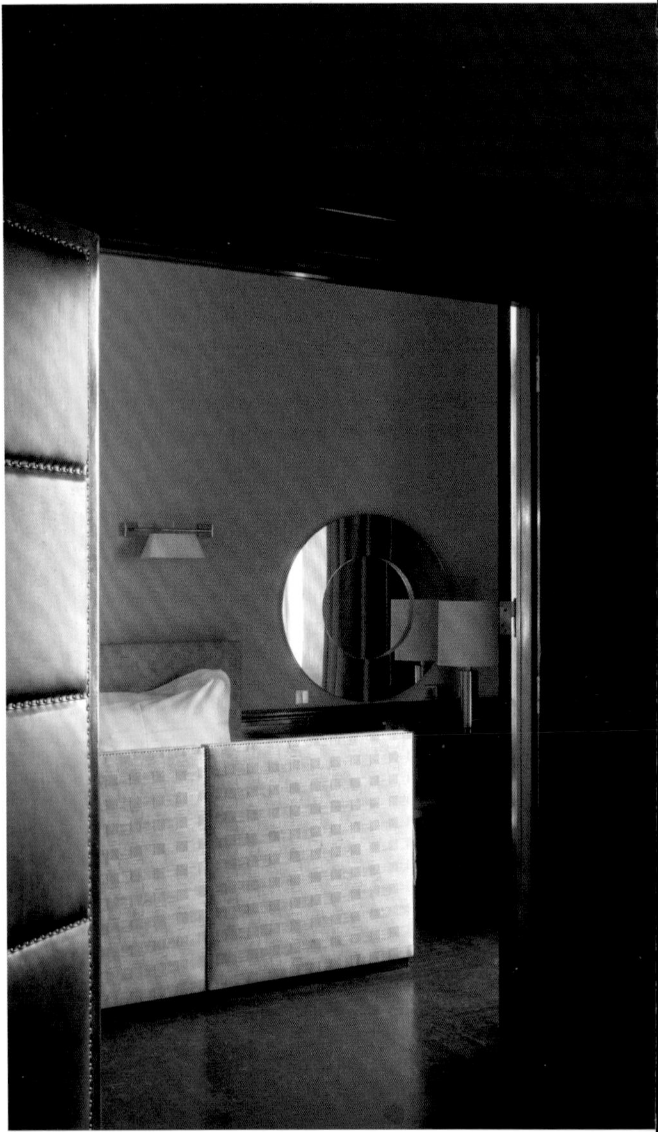

Hotel de Rome
This 1889 building was transformed from a bank into a slick five-star hotel in 2006. Book one of the classically proportioned Historic Suites (pictured), which are former directors' offices and feature the original stucco work. Look out for grenade splinters from WWII still stuck in the wood panelling.
Behrenstrasse 37, T 460 6090, www.hotelderome.com

nhow

Berlin's self-dubbed 'music and lifestyle' hotel, which opened in 2010, sits pretty and pink on the Spree River at the edge of Oberbaum City (see p010). Architect Sergei Tchoban's building may look formal and monolithic from the outside, but its star designer Karim Rashid's biomorphic interiors carry an eye-popping theme throughout, including in the vivid Envy Bar (above). The 304 guest rooms, which follow blue, pink or grey colour schemes, are spacious and futuristic, with curved walls, wave-patterned floors and high-tech sound systems. In keeping with the musical theme, two state-of-the-art recording studios can be found in nhow's Upper Tower, a mirrored block that is cantilevered eight storeys over the river. *Stralauer Allee 3, T 290 2990, www.nhow-hotels.com*

Casa Camper

This is Camper's second hotel, a zinc-clad building of eight floors as clever and unpretentious as the brand's shoes. Throughout the accommodation there's a Berlin-inspired flair for the idiosyncratic and dramatic, from the curtain-draped ceiling in the small lobby to the stage-like space of the Asian restaurant, Dos Palillos (T 2000 3413), designed by Ronan and Erwan Bouroullec. However, the 51 identically decorated rooms, which contain African-hardwood floors and light-filled bathrooms, are tranquil rather than striking. We're particularly fond of the roomy Camper Suite (above). The top-floor Tentiempé café provides guests with free drinks and snacks 24 hours a day to go with its views of Berlin. *Weinmeisterstrasse 1, T 2000 3410, www.casacamper.com/berlin*

Hotel-Pension Dittberner

Due to its Marianne Koplin bedside lamps, raw-silk chaise longue, stucco ceiling and the splendid balcony overlooking a quiet street near the Ku'damm, the Main Suite (above) at the 22-room Dittberner is a lesson in classic West Berlin apartment living. Dittberner might only be a pension, but the elegance of the more sizeable rooms beats the pants off most of the big-name hotels, at a fraction of the price.

The paintings and sculptures throughout lend artistic flair, and the antique lift, which dates to 1911, hints at the history of the place. For a variation on the room service, visit Charlottenburg institution Harry Genenz (T 881 2537), where you can gratefully stock up on *Schwarzwälder kirschtorte* (Black Forest gâteau). *Wielandstrasse 26, T 884 6950, www.hotel-dittberner.de*

24 HOURS

SEE THE BEST OF THE CITY IN JUST ONE DAY

Berlin is a 24-hour city and only your stamina will tell you when it's time to turn in. In summer, weekends start at lunch on Fridays, when Berliners throng to outdoor cafés or beer gardens, such as Prater (Kastanienallee 7-9, T 448 5688), which dates to 1837. If you fancy a stroll, Kreuzberg's Gleisdreieck Park (Möckernstrasse), inaugurated in 2013, is worth a visit, as is the Mauerpark weekend fleamarket (Bernauer Strasse 63-64, T 0176 2925 0021).

The art scene is one of Europe's best. Check out Kreuzkölln's nascent gallery district, specifically Crystal Ball (Schönleinstrasse 7, T 6005 2828); or head over to Tiergarten, where you can view exhibitions at spaces such as Nolan Judin (Potsdamer Strasse 83, T 3940 4840), Wien Lukatsch (Schöneberger Ufer 65, T 2838 5352), which also has a bookshop, and Circle Culture (Potsdamer Strasse 68, T 275 817 846), focusing on urban subculture and street art.

There is a bewildering variety of nightlife, from concerts and clubs to the open-air cinemas and canal-side bacchanals that are a Berlin speciality. Look out for flyers or ask the locals. For those who've partied hard, a favoured tonic is a currywurst at Curry36 (Mehringdamm 36, T 251 7368). Opulent breakfasts are served until late in the afternoon at most cafés – try Nola's am Weinberg (Veteranenstrasse 9, T 4404 0766) – so you can grab some food and well-earned sleep before starting all over again.

For full addresses, see Resources.

10.00 Café Einstein

Berliners do *Frühstück* (breakfast) in style, and the original Café Einstein – not to be confused with the venue at Unter den Linden 42 (T 204 3632) – enjoys a great setting and has a traditional feel. Located, since 1978, inside an 1878 villa of almost mythological status due to its roster of colourful residents and indifference to WWII bombs, Café Einstein has long been a hangout of the city's bohemians and literati. Order a glass of fresh orange juice, coffee and the Viennese breakfast, which includes fluffy rolls and a couple of peeled soft-boiled eggs in a glass. Add butter and seasoning, gather the day's newspapers and make the most of the European coffeehouse atmosphere. On warmer summer mornings, sit outside in the garden.
Kurfürstenstrasse 58, T 0261 5096, www.cafeeinstein.com

12.00 Holocaust Memorial

Nestled between the Brandenburg Gate and Potsdamer Platz is the Memorial to the Murdered Jews of Europe, designed by Peter Eisenman and unveiled in 2005. This impressive monument comprises an undulating field of 2,711 stone monoliths tightly packed into an entire block. You may wonder why Berlin took so long to get round to building it. Yet, when you consider the debate that surrounded the project – from the government rejecting the original designs, to the row about whether it should also honour other Holocaust victims, to the scandal of the contract for the stones' paint being given to a firm whose sister company made the Zyklon B used in the gas chambers – it's a wonder it was ever completed at all.

Cora-Berliner-Strasse 1, T 263 9430, www.holocaust-mahnmal.de

15.30 Sammlung Boros

One of Berlin's most intriguing private art collections is housed inside an imposing 1942 bunker. Postwar, it served as a fruit warehouse before becoming the venue for some notorious techno and fetish parties in the early 1990s. Shut by the authorities, it got a makeover in 2008 when ad mogul Christian Boros installed the highlights of his 700-strong haul of artworks. In a 3,000 sq m space, contemporary works are displayed in 80 boxy concrete rooms. The current exhibition, 'Boros Collection #2', includes eye-catching pieces by Alicja Kwade, Ai Weiwei and Michael Sailstorfer (*Zeit ist Keine Autobahn*, opposite). Access is only possible as part of a guided tour on Thursdays to Sundays, which you can book through the website. Do it well in advance. *Reinhardtstrasse 20, www.sammlung-boros.de*

20.00 Tim Raue

Since departing the Adlon Holding hotel group to launch his eponymous restaurant in 2010, Tim Raue quickly shook up Berlin's fine-dining scene. His daring amalgam of Asian and German cuisine earned him a Michelin star three months after opening, and a second in 2012. Set in an old gallery space that has high ceilings and poured asphalt floors, the restaurant, designed by local architects Ester Bruzkus and Patrick Batek, pays tribute to its environs in artsy Kreuzberg. Expect flashes of colour and a 'sky' of more than 300 light bulbs above a white marble counter in the bar/lounge. The menu's far-flung influences range from Japanese to Thai, resulting in tantalising oddities such as jasmine pigeon with peanut and fig. *Rudi-Dutschke-Strasse 26, T 2593 7930, www.tim-raue.com*

22.00 Prince Charles

Set in a former swimming facility dating to the 1970s, this subterranean club has fuelled the resurgence of the Moritzplatz district. The owners – Nicolas Mönch and Wolfgang Farkas – converted the space, preserving the colourful mosaicked wall in hues of yellow, blue and aquamarine, and developing the interior of the venue around it. Come here on the weekend to knock back cocktails with Berlin's hard-partying set in the sunken pool, and dance beneath a glimmering analogue ceiling installation comprising 500 bulbs that flicker and dim individually. In 2014, the Parker Bowles (it had to be) restaurant opened upstairs, serving trad German cuisine enlivened by international touches, mainly Asian and Latin American.
Prinzenstrasse 85f,
www.princecharlesberlin.com

URBAN LIFE

CAFÉS, RESTAURANTS, BARS AND NIGHTCLUBS

Berlin's nocturnal landscape is smarter these days. The illegal clubs that sprang up in the 1990s – in hard-to-find ruins with little ventilation and few fire exits – have fallen victim to gentrification. Instead, renovated historic buildings are being kitted out with high-end sound systems, as at Gretchen (Obentrautstrasse 19-21, T 2592 2702), Chalet (Vor dem Schlesischen Tor 3, T 6953 6290) and pool turned gallery/club space Stattbad (Gerichtstrasse 65, T 4679 7350). But despite the chic aesthetic, there is still an edge to the nightlife, as you'll discover at artist-collective-run Villa Renate (Alt-Stralau 70, T 2540 1426), in an abandoned house next to the old Wall. Its labyrinth of ramshackle rooms, dark corridors and mezzanines vibrate all weekend to house, disco and techno.

The culinary scene, too, has improved greatly. Since opening in 2009, Reinstoff (see p050) has been showered with awards. It has been joined by the hotspots La Soupe Populaire (opposite), in which Michelin-starred Tim Raue cooks for the common man, Pauly Saal (see p042) and Glass (see p054), where chef Gal Ben Moshe's nouvelle cuisine is a regular talking point. The once-gritty Torstrasse is now restaurant row, lined with stylish bistros such as Noto (No 173, T 2009 5387) and 3 Minutes Sur Mer (No 167, T 6730 2052), as well as clandestine watering holes like Butcher's Bar (No 116), accessed via a telephone booth inside a currywurst joint. *For full addresses, see Resources.*

La Soupe Populaire

The 5,000 sq m cellars of the 1885 Bötzow brewery have been transformed into an exhibition space for contemporary art, the spotlighting casting eerie shapes on the yellow brick and raw concrete. Set on an iron mezzanine within the murky depths is La Soupe Populaire, where chef Tim Raue reimagines comfort food classics such as *Senfei* (boiled eggs in mustard sauce), *Königsberger Klopse* (meatballs) and *Bienenstich* (a vanilla and almond flavour dessert), presented on 1930s Urbino porcelain from the KPM factory. A bespoke menu accompanies each art show and there's a concise choice of mainly German wines. Afterwards go for a cocktail in the adjoining Le Croco Bleu (T 017 7443 2359). Both are open Thursday to Saturday only. *Bötzow Berlin, Prenzlauer Allee 242, T 4431 9680, www.lasoupepopulaire.de*

Pauly Saal

The Jüdische Mädchenschule – an elegant 1930s five-storey brick school designed by Alexander Beer – was returned to the Jewish community in 2009 and converted to its current incarnation by architects Grüntuch Ernst in 2012. It's now home to three galleries, a museum and a pair of restaurants, including the high-end Pauly Saal in the former gymnasium. The interior is adorned with quirky art pieces, Murano chandeliers and ceramic wall tiles. A large red-and-white missile by Cosima von Bonin is mounted above the open kitchen, where chef Michael Höpfl has been garnering acclaim for his elevated take on regional and seasonal fare. Enjoy dishes such as Pomeranian ox entrecôte or suckling pig and black pudding tortellini.
Auguststrasse 11-13, T 3300 6070, www.paulysaal.com

Luzia

Istanbul-bred brothers Kaan and Yasin Müjdeci have helped put a contemporary sheen on Oranienstrasse, Kreuzberg's lived-in boozy strip, with their concept store Voo (see p085) and, a few doors down, the urbane late-night hangout Luzia. Opened in 2007, the bar is popular with twentysomething professionals, savvy tourists and Mitte types in search of debauchery, who pack in nightly between semi-exposed brick walls adorned with gilded mirrors and murals by local street artist Chin Chin. Luzia turns into a bit of a meat market after 1am and is preferable during the day in warmer months, when the floor-to-ceiling glass facade slides away and the outdoor tables are perfect for coffee, cake and people-watching. *Oranienstrasse 34, T 8179 9958, www.luzia.tc*

Típica

Until recently, a common complaint in
Berlin concerned the scarcity of decent
Mexican cuisine. Then, starting with the
2009 opening of Maria Bonita (Danziger
Strasse 33), came a new wave of venues
serving up authentic south-of-the-border
grub. Típica is the chicest of the bunch, in
a light-filled space designed by architects
KLM, who drew on Latin colour schemes
with clean white walls and hints of coral
and sand. Owner/chef René Brembach
had no previous restaurant experience
when he launched Típica in 2010, but
you wouldn't know it. Try the *tacos al
pastor*: grilled pork in a chilli-achiote
salsa served in a tortilla. Wash it down
with another Mexican original, a sweet
hibiscus-infused *agua fresca*.
*Rosenstrasse 19, T 2509 9440,
www.tipica.de*

Lokal

At the forefront of Berlin's farm-to-table movement, Lokal, which opened in 2011, is the follow-up to its now defunct but hugely successful predecessor, Kantine, a temporary restaurant in the office space of architect David Chipperfield. At Lokal, Berliner Maren Thimm and her American partner, chef Gary Hoopengardner, serve up regional fare which is bought in from the surrounding areas and forged into a menu that changes daily. Adventurous diners will be pleased by Hoopengardner's fondness for game and innards, which are prepared to perfection. The modern-rustic interior was conceived by local designer Katja Buchholz, and includes handcrafted timber furniture and hanging lamps fashioned from glass fish traps.
Linienstrasse 160, T 2844 9500,
www.lokal-berlin.blogspot.com

Alpenstueck

The name translates as 'a piece of the Alps' and this venue certainly has a calm, rarefied atmosphere. The pared-down interior by local firm BFS Design combines stacked logs with cool grey tones and balanced lighting. The food is hearty but contemporary mountain fare, made using local produce. *Gartenstrasse 9, T 2175 1646, www.alpenstueck.de*

Reinstoff

Less than a year after opening in 2009, this 35-seat restaurant, set inside a red-brick former fire station and run by chef Daniel Achilles, won a Michelin star. It gained a second in 2011. Achilles divides his edible creations into two menus: 'quite near', comprising regional classics using local ingredients, and 'far away', which is more experimental. The food is presented within an intimate but theatrical setting, designed by architects Bolwin Wulf, that plays dramatically with dark and light. Low-level lighting is used to accentuate artfully plated dishes, such as sea bream with stone crab and sea infusion, whereas the rest of the space remains cloaked in darkness. Reinstoff is open for dinner only, from Tuesday to Saturday.
Edison Höfe, Schlegelstrasse 26c, T 3088 1214, www.reinstoff.eu

Lava

Renate and Andreas Hoffmann's Italian restaurant, Lavanderia Vecchia (T 6272 2152), has a months-long waiting list. So, in 2012, they opened Lava in the same block. It mimics a 1920s Weimar small-business set-up – retail (a deli) facing the street, plus a living space and a back room for entertaining. It's been given a dose of the surreal via a chequerboard floor, a stream of pink fibreoptics flowing through a bath and, in the Grüner Salon, cracked green paint and chandeliers on the floor. Lunch is simple but, by night, Lava adopts a creative Mediterranean approach in its five-course set menu and à la carte options, which change every few weeks and include the likes of grilled lamb with miso aubergine purée.
Flughafenstrasse 46, T 2234 6908, www.lavaberlin.wordpress.com

House Of Weekend

Established nightspot House Of Weekend attracts an international crowd. Located in the former Haus des Reisens (see p064), designed by architects Robertneun and renovated in 2014, it is regularly used as a venue for vernissage and after-show parties during Fashion Week. On summer evenings, take the rather claustrophobic lift up to the 17th-floor roof garden, which has low-level bench seating and top views across Alexanderplatz to the sky-piercing Fernsehturm (see p015), for a sundowner BBQ prepared by the Michelin-starred chef Stefan Hartmann. After 11pm, make your way down to the dancefloor (above). The playlist covers house, techno and electro, and in true Berlin style, clubbers here tend not to leave the place any time before 6am.
Alexanderstrasse 7,
www.week-end-berlin.de

Glass

Set up in 2012 by gregarious Israeli chef Gal Ben Moshe, who often works the floor, Glass provides imaginative fine-dining and a refreshingly informal vibe. A former fitness studio in a residential block has been put through its paces by Mexico City architects Christoph Zeller and Ingrid Moye. A neon sign draws you to the glass cube, and inside it's all about the curtain of metallised polyester that reflects both light and movement – as well as a distinct lack of starched tablecloths. The six- or eight-course menu changes almost daily, but dishes, whether a veal cheek ravioli 'explosion' or scallops with horseradish, apple and lobster butter, always showcase innovation and attention to detail – many are inspired by a Berlin-related theme. *Uhlandstrasse 195, T 5471 0861, www.glassberlin.de*

The Grand

Boasting antique paintings, marble floors and leather booths, this restaurant, event space and bar lives up to its name. The building was previously a school for underprivileged children, dating to 1842, and is now under historic preservation. Interiors mix classicism with some very Berlin touches, including rough walls in fading colours, and a steel chandelier by film-set designer Martina Brünner. In the restaurant (above), chef Tilo Roth specialises in barbecuing fine cuts of meat on a grill that reaches 800°C. The ground-floor bar resembles an explorer's cabinet, displaying animal drawings on the walls and wooden crocodiles in glass cases, and the club DJs play electro and house to a stylish crowd on weekends. *Hirtenstrasse 4, T 278 909 955, www.the-grand-berlin.com*

Tin

On a cobbled street overlooking Landwehr canal, Tin (formerly Tin Tin) is a dash of high style in laidback Kreuzkölln. The restaurant and bar's open-plan interior features concrete walls and tables, a hammered-metal counter and dozens of bare light bulbs, all put together by design firm Karhard, the team behind the interior of Panorama Bar (T 2936 0210). If it sounds a bit grey and heavy, it's not: the ambience is as warm as the friendly service, and as varied as the food. On offer are seasonal and local dishes, which include Caesar salad with strips of lamb, a Kreuzberg-style anchovy platter, and an extensive cocktail list. Tin also opens for lunch in summer, and has a front patio from which diners can observe the paddle boats floating by on the canal.
Paul-Linke-Ufer 39-40, T 4882 6894, www.tin-berlin.com

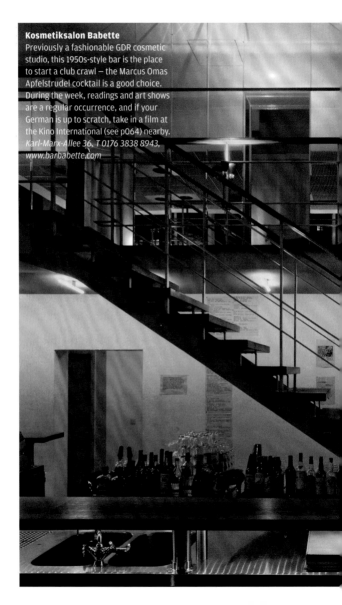

Kosmetiksalon Babette
Previously a fashionable GDR cosmetic
studio, this 1950s-style bar is the place
to start a club crawl – the Marcus Omas
Apfelstrudel cocktail is a good choice.
During the week, readings and art shows
are a regular occurrence, and if your
German is up to scratch, take in a film at
the Kino International (see p064) nearby.
*Karl-Marx-Allee 36, T 0176 3838 8943,
www.barbabette.com*

Borchardt

The social status of being seated at one of the niche tables in Borchardt is not to be underestimated. The restaurant of choice for Berlin's celeb set is not only loved for its *plateaux de fruits de mer* and chilled riesling but also for the fine dramaturgy of its seating allocation: tourists and potential stalkers are placed firmly front of house. Decor follows the style of a classic French brasserie, with marble pillars and golden mosaics. The menu changes daily, but retains a focus on regional dishes, including a lovely Wiener schnitzel and a delicious beef steak with mixed salad, and asparagus is a speciality when it's in season. Afterwards, go for a cocktail, and a wall full of fashion nudes, at the nearby Newton Bar (T 2029 5421).
Französische Strasse 47, T 8188 6262, www.borchardt-restaurant.de

Bar Tausend

In the arches under the Friedrichstrasse S-Bahn, Bar Tausend shudders with the weight of each passing train. Yet this is far from a grungy dive, especially since adding a clandestine jewel box of a restaurant, Cantina, behind its happening bar in 2009. In charge of the tiny open kitchen is one of Berlin's most creative Asian chefs, Duc Ngo. From his culinary HQ he serves up Latin-Asian-inspired dishes such as

Peruvian *tiradito* (similar to ceviche), miso cod, and sashimi salad. There's also a Japanese-influenced cocktail list – try the Oscaland, which blends sake with basil syrup and jasmine tea. Book a table for about 10.30pm, when the restaurant starts to get going as the art collectors, Russian models and international socialites roll up. *Schiffbauerdamm 11, T 2758 2070, www.tausendberlin.com*

INSIDERS' GUIDE

PHILIPP SCHÖPFER AND DANIEL KLAPSING, DESIGNERS

As the dual founders of design studio 45 Kilo, Philipp Schöpfer (opposite, left) and Daniel Klapsing create custom-made Bauhaus-influenced furniture. Most of their favourite places in Berlin reflect a preference for the pared down. Their drinking den of choice, Buck and Breck (Brunnenstrasse 177), consists of a single room, almost entirely taken up by a counter, around which guests sip cocktails. 'You have to ring the bell to get in,' explains Schöpfer. For inspiration, they head to Johann König (Dessauer Strasse 6-7, T 2610 3080), a 'huge space that offers artists the ability to show large installations', or Appel Design Gallery (Torstrasse 114, T 3251 8160), which specialises in midcentury furniture. 'There aren't many design galleries that have a gallery atmosphere,' observes Klapsing. 'Here, it's nothing more than the actual pieces.'

Fans of Mitte's independent retail scene, the pair shop at Soto (Torstrasse 72, T 2576 2070), a men's concept store stocking labels such as Our Legacy, and Marron (Augustrasse 77-78, T 2809 4878), a furniture, design and accessories boutique. Both also relish trips to the ramen restaurant Cocolo (Gipsstrasse 3). When it comes to clubbing, instead of queuing to get into techno temple Berghain (Wriezener Bahnhof, T 2936 0210), they hit the venue at 5pm on Sunday. 'Looking at all the people who stayed for two nights in a row is quite interesting, and a little embarrassing,' says Schöpfer. *For full addresses, see Resources.*

ARCHITOUR
A GUIDE TO BERLIN'S ICONIC BUILDINGS

You can't beat Berlin for its panoply of 20th-century architecture, from Bauhaus to new brutalist, with all shades of ugly, charming and ridiculous in-between. Its various architectural showpieces include Hans Scharoun's Philharmonie (Herbert-von-Karajan-Strasse 1, T 254 880); Foster + Partners' revamped Reichstag (Platz der Republik 1, T 2273 2152); Daniel Libeskind's dramatic Jewish Museum (Lindenstrasse 9-14, T 2599 3300), to which the architect added on an education centre in 2012; Mies van der Rohe's Neue Nationalgalerie (Potsdamer Strasse 50, T 266 424 242); and the Fernsehturm (see p015). The capital has so many gems, from Peter Behrens' AEG Turbine Factory (Huttenstrasse 12-19) to Foster + Partners' Philological Library (Habelschwerdter Allee 45, T 8385 8888), that we can only list the highlights of the highlights.

Although the city was reunified more than 20 years ago, it's still intriguing to compare GDR and FRG architecture. For example, the Stalinist Karl-Marx-Allee, which leads to Hermann Henselmann's Internationalist buildings – encompassing the Haus des Reisens (Alexanderplatz 7) and Kino International (Karl-Marx-Allee 33, T 2475 6011) – contrasts with the Western equivalent, the not as bombastic but still inspiring structures of the 1957 International Building Exhibition (Interbau) in Hansaviertel, which includes work by Oscar Niemeyer, Walter Gropius and Werner Düttmann. *For full addresses, see Resources.*

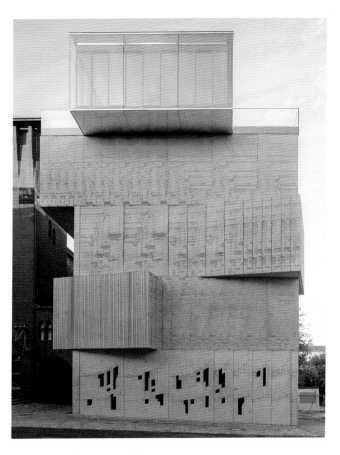

Museum for Architectural Drawing

A 2013 addition to the Pfefferberg cultural complex built out of the shell of an 1848 brewery, this museum by Sergei Tchoban and Sergei Kuznetsov aims to reawaken an interest in draftsmanship and doesn't disappoint. The yellowy concrete facade emulates parchment and is covered with architectural sketches in relief, while the irregularly stacked floors resemble open drawers. The collection includes blueprints from 18th-century architects such as Giacomo Quarenghi, right through to sketches by Frank Gehry; there are also temporary exhibitions. Book a tour to see the engraved nutwood panelling in the library and the views from the glass box and terrace on the roof. Open 2pm to 7pm; 1pm to 5pm on Saturdays and Sundays. *Christinenstrasse 18a, T 4373 9090, www.tchoban-foundation.de*

Haus der Kulturen der Welt

Designed by the US architect Hugh
Stubbins and completed in 1957, this
former conference centre is known
as the 'pregnant oyster' because of its
shell-shaped concrete roof. Restored
in 2007, it's now a contemporary arts
space. The pool outside is home to a
1984 Henry Moore bronze, *Big Butterfly*.
*John-Foster-Dulles-Allee 10,
T 3978 7175, www.hkw.de*

DZ Bank Building

Restrained by planning regulations in a historically sensitive location on Pariser Platz, Frank Gehry's first build in Berlin saves its deconstructivist surprises for the interior. Finished in 2001, the deceptively plain limestone facade of the former DG Bank gives way to a writhing fish-like form (a common inspiration for Gehry) in glass, wood and metal that dominates the central atrium (above). The shiny, curvaceous belly of the 'whale' houses the AXICA conference hall, part of what is now an office and residential block. In 2013, Gehry won the commission to design Germany's tallest residential tower, in Alexanderplatz. Set to soar 150m over 39 floors, the cream, stone-clad structure will turn on its axis at the top 12 storeys, and is due for completion in 2017.
Pariser Platz 3

Neues Museum

Closed for 70 years after being bombed during WWII, the Neues Museum finally reopened, after much effort and €233m-worth of funding, to great fanfare in 2009. And although the iconic 'Bust of Nefertiti' is still drawing crowds, it is the building's clever renovation by David Chipperfield that has satisfied the critics. The British architect and his team did not merely reconstruct what was here or clean up the fragments, they created rooms where one can still see and feel Friedrich August Stüler's original design. In the case of elements that had to be replaced, like the main stairway, Chipperfield rebuilt the original but used different materials, such as pre-cast concrete, to give the space both a modern look and a ghostly feel. *Bodestrasse 1-3, T 266 424 242, www.neues-museum.de*

Labels 2

The city has started to augment the banks of the meandering Spree River, slowly lining it with architectural jewels. One such example is the showy Labels 2, which opened in 2010 and is designed by the Swiss architects HHF. Behind the wave-patterned concrete facade, inspired by the Spree and by the arched windows of a neighbouring warehouse, lies a complex of fashion showrooms and event spaces (Berlin is attempting to bring international attention to its youthful and innovative fashion scene). Also worthy of note is the structure's clever eco-friendly design, which incorporates a network of tubes that contain water from the river, heated during the winter and cooled in summer. This system reduces energy consumption by an impressive 40 per cent.

Stralauer Allee 12, T 8906 4210

SHOPPING

THE BEST RETAIL THERAPY AND WHAT TO BUY

The Scheunenviertel area offers a host of independent boutiques centred around Neue and Alte Schönhauser Strasse. Don't skip the side streets here as they house some real gems. Mulackstrasse is fertile territory for up-and-coming retailers – womenswear at Schwarzhogerzeil (No 28, T 2887 3868) and stationery at RSVP (No 14, T 2809 4644). Nearby, seek out the accessories at Hecking (Gormannstrasse 8-9, T 2804 7528), ethical menswear at Atelier Akeef (see p078), rare and vintage furnishings in the quirky 10119 (Linienstrasse 106, T 2809 4714) and fashion at the independent boutiques Adddress (Weinmeisterstrasse 12-14, T 2887 3434) and Anuschka Hoevener (Linienstrasse 196, T 4431 9299). Or do all your shopping under one roof at popular concept stores Andreas Murkudis (see p074) and Happy Shop (Torstrasse 67, T 2900 9501).

There are two major arteries for big fashion brands. Out west on Kurfürstendamm, Jil Sander (No 185, T 886 7020) sits beside other global names, as well as private design showrooms such as Galerie Ulrich Fiedler (opposite), while up the road is the grand dame KaDeWe (Tauentzienstrasse 21-24, T 21 210). Friedrichstrasse, in the former East, is home to Galeries Lafayette (No 76-78, T 209 480) and the elegant covered arcade Quartier 206 (No 71, T 2094 6500), which contains the pioneering emporium Departmentstore Quartier 206, designed by style guru Anne Maria Jagdfeld.
For full addresses, see Resources.

Galerie Ulrich Fiedler

After 20 years in Cologne, Ulrich Fiedler moved his showroom to Berlin in 2008. Specialising in the European avant-garde (Bauhaus, De Stijl, French modernism) from the 1920s up to the 1950s and 1960s, his collection contains furniture by Alvar Aalto, Marcel Breuer, Gerrit Rietveld and Mies van der Rohe, as well as metalware, ceramics, graphic design and photography. In 2013, the gallery relocated to the first floor of an art nouveau building, accessed by elegant stairs. The space has a classic Berlin apartment feel, all herringbone floors, whitewashed walls and stuccoed ceilings. In an adjacent room, displays explore the influence of movements such as Arts and Crafts or designers like Karl Friedrich Schinkel. By appointment only. *Mommsenstrasse 59, T 3309 4010, www.ulrichfiedler.com*

Andreas Murkudis

Although Mitte is still ground zero for high-end boutique shopping, the 2011 opening of Andreas Murkudis' unisex fashion emporium on the resurgent Potsdamer Strasse has given Berlin's style-set ample occasion to head west. Murkudis elicited the assistance of local architects Gonzalez Haase to fill these 1,000 sq m digs – housed in a former printing press – and within you'll find a carefully curated but diverse range of items, from Margiela ankle boots to Nymphenburg porcelain and scarves by Neri Firenze. Exhibitions are sometimes held, local sunglasses firm Mykita has its own concession, and there's a sunken level in which furniture by German brand e15 is sold. Closed Sundays.
Potsdamer Strasse 81e, T 680 798 306, www.andreasmurkudis.com

Lunettes Selection

In 2006, frustrated by the difficulties of sourcing stylish vintage eyewear in the city, Uta Geyer decided to launch her own boutique, Lunettes, in Prenzlauer Berg (T 4471 8050). A second, flagship outlet on Torstrasse opened in 2010, and the understated shop carries an excellent crop of classic frames by brands such as Algha and Cazal, which are kept in a large 1950s wooden commode. Directly across from it, an old-school eye-test chart hangs on the white wall. In 2010, Geyer unveiled the Lunettes Kollektion, a line of vintage-influenced spectacles, which includes the 'Jean Claude' (above), €259. Everything in this range is handmade in Italy and sold in cases that are inspired by soap and chocolate boxes from the 1920s. *Torstrasse 172, T 2021 5216, www.lunettes-selection.com*

Atelier Akeef

Alan Sommerville and Michael Ashley's Atelier Akeef is the city's first menswear boutique with a 100 per cent commitment to fair trade and ecological brands. Even the eye-catching masculine interior has been built with sustainability in mind; the floors and display units are made from upcycled timber, and the deep-blue clay walls and burgundy iron girders have been coloured using non-toxic substances. The tightly curated range of intelligent brands includes organic jumpers from Knowledge Cotton Apparel, Fair Wear denim by Kings of Indigo and trainers from Faguo, which plants a tree for each pair sold. Accessories include Millican's canvas bags, alongside grooming products such as nutrient-rich Ambre botanicals, handmade in small batches, deploying pure, natural sources. *Max-Beer-Strasse 31, www.atelierakeef.com*

P & T

Founded by Jens de Gruyter, nephew of a tea trader, P & T (Paper and Tea) aims to elevate tea appreciation into the same league as wine or coffee. The mostly white interior was a collaborative effort with product designer Fabian von Ferrari, and the museum-like presentation stands have drawers that enable customers to see and smell loose leaves of various oxidations, beneath clusters of contemporary Chinese lanterns hung in abstract wire grids. There are accompanying texts to explain each batch's provenance, characteristics and production processes, as well as tasting stations for sampling. The shelves are lined with teapots and cups in stoneware, glass and porcelain – these often limited-edition pieces are created in conjunction with internationally known artists.
Bleibtreustrasse 4, www.paperandtea.com

Sprüth Magers
This sprawling gallery, set in a former
dance hall, was opened by art-world
figures Monika Sprüth and Philomene
Magers in 2008. Artists such as Andrea
Zittel ('Pattern of Habit', pictured), Cindy
Sherman and Andreas Gursky continue
to exhibit, and the venue also has a DVD
shop, Image Movement, which screens
arthouse films on a regular basis.
Oranienburger Strasse 18, T 2888 4030

LOCAL VODKA
BY
Our / Berlin
AM FLUTGRABEN 2
12435 BERLIN

VODKA WITH A FLAVOR PRODUCED FROM OUR LOCAL RECIPE
LOCALLY PRODUCED · HAND BOTTLED IN BERLIN
ENJOY RESPONSIBLY

Alc. 37,5% vol. 350ml

Simon&Me

Created in 2008 by 18-year-olds Simon Freund and Alex Rückheim, gents' lifestyle label Simon&Me underwent a conceptual revamp in 2013, although it retained the minimalist aesthetic. Its slogan – Made In Germany – is stamped on everything, and the ethos extends to the space itself, which has bespoke furniture and a stucco ceiling that's a nod to the craftsmanship on offer. Each item has been meticulously designed, and most of the clothes and accessories are limited edition. Books and boutique alcohol, like Our/Berlin vodka (above), €15 for 350ml, are stocked too. Many products are customisable in store, which is open Saturdays (12-6pm) or by appointment; Simon&Me is also on sale at Supergrau (T 7551 7004) and Voo Store (see p085). *Fidicinstrasse 17, T 6396 0563, www.simonandme.com*

Apartment

To find this subterranean, cutting-edge fashion boutique you have to enter an unmarked door, go through an empty, all-white storefront and then down a dark spiral staircase. Finally, you arrive in a cave-like narrow space, lit with bars of fluorescent light, displaying a mix of rather well-edited cultish fashion items for both men and women, including a suede biker jacket by Rick Owens and a leather dress by Gareth Pugh. We have also heard that you can bargain with the salespeople here. There are myriad other boutiques to explore in the area, and when you fancy a break, join the Mitte trendies at Café Oliv (T 8920 6540), which serves health-conscious sustenance and locally roasted coffee in a stylish interior. *Memhardstrasse 8, T 2804 2251, www.apartmentberlin.de*

Voo Store

Located within a former locksmiths in a *Hinterhof* (back courtyard) on Kreuzberg's still gritty Oranienstrasse, Voo combines hipster street style with sustainability and a preference for small, innovative manufacturers. Opened in 2010, it hosts brands such as Acne, Carin Wester and local label Don't Shoot the Messengers, as well as selling surprising one-off items like Hudsalva, the lip balm of the Swedish military. There's a set of turntables for DJs to spin, and owners Yasin and Kaan Müjdeci, of bar Luzia (see p044), utilise the space as a venue for exhibitions, readings and concerts. In 2013, Voo unveiled another attraction – Shawn Barber and Chris Onton's on-site café, Companion Coffee (T 176 6344 6225). *Oranienstrasse 24, T 6165 1119, www.vooberlin.com*

Objets Trouvés

A stockist of industrial design and vintage furnishings, Objets Trouvés built on the runaway success of its original Prenzlauer Berg store and opened this spacious outlet in 2014 on the border of Mitte and the up-and-coming Wedding district. The name translates as 'found objects', and owners Magdalena and Robert Hohberg travel Europe searching for pieces that tell a story. Highlights include wood-and-glass medicine cabinets from the 1920s, original Egon Eiermann and Harry Bertoia chairs, and timber benches from Prague topped with cognac-coloured leather. The owners are also dab hands at upcycling, turning old gym equipment or theatre-set lighting into covetable pieces for the home. The pretty grey-and-rose facade provides little clue as to the minimal interior and often functional aesthetic behind it.
Brunnenstrasse 169, T 016 3181 0985, www.objets-trouves-berlin.de

SPORTS AND SPAS

WORK OUT, CHILL OUT OR JUST WATCH

Being flat, Berlin is a haven for cyclists, and an extensive network of paths makes this the perfect way to get around town. In the summer, the city is dotted with Deutsche Bahn's distinctive hire bikes (T 069 4272 7722, www.callabike-interaktiv.de), which you can pick up and ride, using your mobile phone to pay.

Per capita, Berlin has a high proportion of public swimming pools (see p094), including some of the most well-designed and equipped in Europe. Opening times, however, are at best erratic and at worst annoying. Otherwise, the clean lakes surrounding the city offer bathing and sailing in summer, or skating in winter. The Olympiastadion (opposite), built for the 1936 Games, is mightily impressive; you can watch local football team Hertha play here.

Most 'wellness' areas are inside the main hotels: Club Olympus Spa & Fitness in the Grand Hyatt (see p016); the sumptuous Spa de Rome (T 460 609 1160) at Hotel de Rome (see p026); and the Susanne Kaufmann Spa, offering a pool, a sauna and treatments influenced by Chinese medicine, at Das Stue (see p020). For styling in sleek surrounds, flamboyant French hairdresser Viktor Leske's Scheunenviertel salon (Joachimstrasse 8, T 2790 8487) was given an industrial aesthetic by local studio Karhard, who introduced dark wood, exposed concrete and stainless-steel mirrors curving down from the ceiling. It's quintessentially Berlin.
For full addresses, see Resources.

Olympiastadion

This iconic oval structure, designed by Werner March, may owe its external form to its National Socialist past, but inside it is a superb example of modern stadium design. Initially built as the main venue for the 1936 Olympics, it was renovated between 2000 and 2004 by Hamburg architects von Gerkan, Marg und Partner (GMP) in preparation for hosting the 2006 FIFA World Cup Final. The limestone facade is deceptive; the interior is scooped out and more than half of the stadium lies underground. GMP lowered the pitch by a further 2.65m to increase the overall capacity to 74,649, and added a delicate, translucent roof membrane, which slots seamlessly into the original structure. Check out the view from the 77m belltower. *Olympischer Platz 3, T 3068 8100, www.olympiastadion-berlin.de*

Velodrom
French architect Dominique Perrault's circular indoor velodrome opened in 1997 and nestles mostly below ground under a shimmering metal roof. Capable of holding 12,000 spectators, it is used more for concerts than cycling. Head next door to see the equally stylish pool complex, one of the largest in Europe.
Paul-Heyse-Strasse 26, T 443 045,
www.velodrom.de

Schon geduscht?

Liquidrom

At Berlin's clubbiest spa, immerse yourself in electronic or classical music, performed live or selected by DJs, while floating in a warm, darkened 'sound pool' surrounded by colourful light projections (opposite). The futuristic complex has large, stylish relaxation rooms as well a dome-shaped inner sanctum, and is the work of GMP, who also designed Berlin's huge, greenhouse-like Hauptbahnhof (see p009). Four types of massage include a Balinese herbal ball treatment, and there are three saunas, three pools (plunge pool, above) and a steam bath. The crowd is an interesting assortment: in the Japanese onsen pool or Himalaya salt sauna expect to see couples relaxing next to hungover folks who have clearly arrived straight from the dancefloor. *Möckernstrasse 10, T 258 007 820, www.liquidrom-berlin.de*

Badeschiff

What started off as an urban-regeneration experiment to enliven Berlin's neglected river area turned into one of the city's favourite R&R venues. Opened in 2004, the Badeschiff (bathing ship) is essentially an old barge on the Spree that was refitted as a heated pool by Spanish firm AMP in collaboration with local architect Gil Wilk and artist Susanne Lorenz. The wood decking and docklands ambience, as well as the regular events and DJs, make it a perfect post-industrial venue for a lazy afternoon, particularly in the height of summer. During the winter, cocoon-like coverings (above) ensure that the pool, bar, sauna and massage area are kept at a cosy temperature, in direct contrast to the ice-floe-filled river on which they sit.
Eichenstrasse 4, T 533 2030,
www.badeschiff.de

ESCAPES

WHERE TO GO IF YOU WANT TO LEAVE TOWN

It's hard to run out of things to do in Berlin, but if you do need respite from the city, you can take a train to almost anywhere in Europe from the Hauptbahnhof (see p009). Szczecin in Poland is only 140km away and is a popular excursion, but you don't have to cross the border – options include Hamburg (90 minutes via the high-speed link), Leipzig (just over an hour) and Dresden (about two hours). A visit to Dessau (opposite) is an inspiring trip back to the engine room of the Bauhaus movement. The sandy-shored lakes on the capital's outskirts and in surrounding Brandenburg are ideal for nature lovers. In summer, Strandbad Wannsee (see p100), and Werbellinsee, an hour north, are lovely, and in winter, packing a hot toddy and going ice-skating there is a great day out.

Potsdam, the former summer residence of the Hohenzollerns, was wrecked by WWII and East German road planners, but it's now a well-restored, attractive town, located 25km south-west of Berlin. In summer, the crowds at Sanssouci Palace (Maulbeerallee, T 033 1969 4200) are a drag, but Erich Mendelsohn's expressionist Einsteinturm (see p101) justifies the journey and the trek through the Albert Einstein Science Park. Also well worth seeking out in Potsdam is Rudy Ricciotti's interior for the Nikolaisaal concert hall (Wilhelm-Staab-Strasse 10-11, T 033 1288 8828), a rare piece of contemporary architecture hidden behind a baroque facade. *For full addresses, see Resources.*

Bauhaus Building, Dessau

Only an hour and a half from Berlin, the city of Dessau should be a pilgrimage for all modernism fans. It was the home of the Bauhaus movement between 1925 and 1932, and founder Walter Gropius' building rapidly became an iconic structure. The architecture and its historical significance motivated UNESCO to add the Bauhaus Building and the nearby Masters' Houses to its World Heritage list in 1996. You can book twice-daily tours (in German only) to see the interiors, including the auditorium and the director's room. Of the remaining Masters' Houses, both Oskar Schlemmer's former residence (Ebertallee 67) and the beautifully restored living quarters of Paul Klee and Wassily Kandinsky (overleaf; Ebertallee 69-71) are essential viewing. *Gropiusallee 38, T 034 0650 8250, www.bauhaus-dessau.de*

Kandinsky/Klee House, Dessau

Strandbad Wannsee

If you have a hankering for messing about in boats, you don't have to travel far. The Wannsee is a series of lakes connected to the city's second-largest river, the Havel, surrounded by forest. It is located south-west of Berlin near Potsdam (opposite), half an hour away by train. Strandbad Wannsee is one of the longest inland lidos in Europe, with a beach stretching 1,275m. Here you can hire rowing boats or kick back on one of the distinctive wicker chairs (above), which can be rented for €8 a day. The beach can get rather crowded; sailing is more relaxing but you'll need to befriend a local with a yacht. If you've got the time, catch the ferry to Pfaueninsel (Peacock Island), where King Friedrich Wilhelm II of Prussia's white palace dates from 1797 and is set in landscaped gardens along with a number of other historical monuments.

Einsteinturm, Potsdam

This curious tower, completed in 1921, was designed by Erich Mendelsohn for the astronomer Erwin Finlay-Freundlich to observe the sun and to substantiate Einstein's Theory of Relativity. Legend has it that Mendelsohn took Einstein on a tour of the tower to get his impression. The physicist's one-word review was 'organic'. In fact, the building was so experimental that it only remains in place thanks to constant renovation work, as the early concrete from which it was built is not up to the structural task, so visit before gravity gets the upper hand. Afterwards, make your way to Restaurant Juliette (T 033 1270 1791) in Potsdam's Dutch quarter to enjoy classic French fare in comfortable surroundings.
Albert Einstein Science Park,
Telegrafenberg, T 033 174 990, www.aip.de

GfZK, Leipzig
The city of Leipzig in Saxony has a cultural tradition encompassing art, book fairs, education and JS Bach. Its politically minded GfZK (gallery of contemporary art) puts on exhibitions and funds projects that aim to examine the role of art in a post-socialist country. The café/bar is lively both day and night.
Karl-Tauchnitz-Strasse 9–11,
T 034 114 0810, www.gfzk.de

NOTES
SKETCHES AND MEMOS

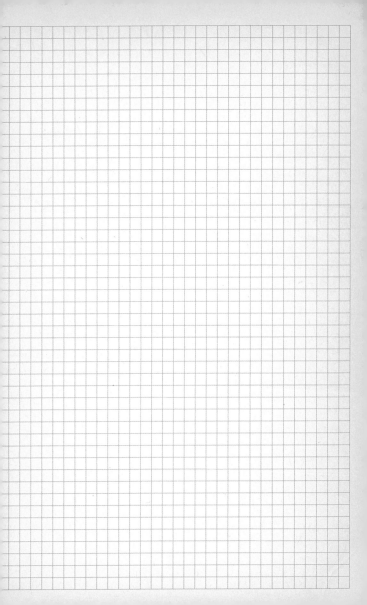

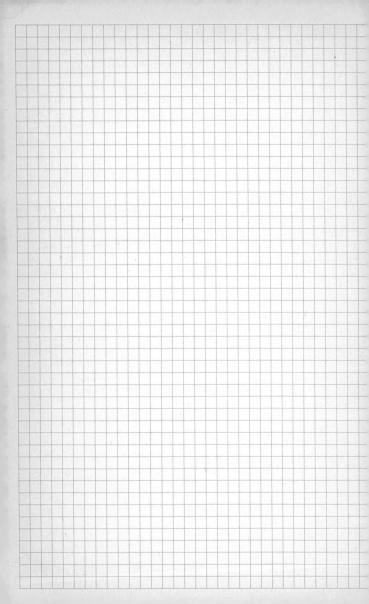

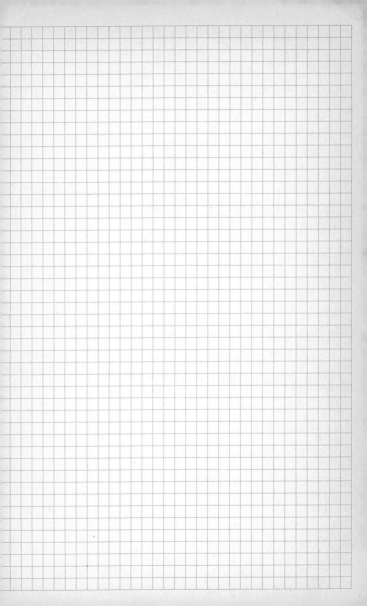

RESOURCES

CITY GUIDE DIRECTORY

A

Adddress 072
Weinmeisterstrasse 12-14
T 2887 3434
www.adddress.de

AEG Turbine Factory 064
Huttenstrasse 12-19

Alpenstueck 048
Gartenstrasse 9
T 2175 1646
www.alpenstueck.de

Andreas Murkudis 074
Potsdamer Strasse 81e
T 680 798 306
www.andreasmurkudis.com

Anuschka Hoevener 072
Linienstrasse 196
T 4431 9299
www.anuschkahoevener.de

Apartment 084
Memhardstrasse 8
T 2804 2251
www.apartmentberlin.de

Appel Design Gallery 062
Torstrasse 114
T 3251 8160
www.appel-design.com

Atelier Akeef 078
Max-Beer-Strasse 31
www.atelierakeef.com

B

Badeschiff 094
Eichenstrasse 4
T 533 2030
www.badeschiff.de

Bahnhof Zoologischer Garten 009
Hardenbergplatz 13
www.bahnhof.de

Bar Tausend 061
Schiffbauerdamm 11
T 2758 2070
www.tausendberlin.com

Bauhaus Building 097
Gropiusallee 38
Dessau
T 034 0650 8250
www.bauhaus-dessau.de

BCC 009
Alexanderstrasse 11
T 2380 6750
www.bcc-berlin.de

Berghain 062
Wriezener Bahnhof
T 2936 0210
www.berghain.de

Berlin Wall Memorial 009
Bernauer Strasse 119
T 467 986 666
www.berliner-mauer-gedenkstaette.de

Borchardt 060
Französische Strasse 47
T 8188 6262
www.borchardt-restaurant.de

Buck and Breck 062
Brunnenstrasse 177
www.buckandbreck.com

Butcher's Bar 040
Torstrasse 116
www.butcher-berlin.de

C

Café Einstein 033
Kurfürstenstrasse 58
T 0261 5096
www.cafeeinstein.com

HOTELS
ADDRESSES AND ROOM RATES

Hotel Amano 022
Room rates:
double, from €80
Augustrasse 43
T 809 4150
www.hotel-amano.com

Casa Camper 029
Room rates:
double, from €195;
Camper Suite, from €255
Weinmeisterstrasse 1
T 2000 3410
www.casacamper.com/berlin

Cosmo 016
Room rates:
double, from €110
Spittelmarkt 13
T 5858 2222
www.cosmo-hotel.de

Hotel-Pension Dittberner 030
Room rates:
double, from €80;
Main Suite, €140
Wielandstrasse 26
T 884 6950
www.hotel-dittberner.de

Gorki Apartments 018
Room rates:
double, from €170;
H Schuhmacher, €200;
Penthouse 2, from €750;
Penthouse 1, from €900
Weinbergersweg 25
T 4849 6480
www.gorkiapartments.de

Grand Hyatt 016
Room rates:
double, from €195
Marlene-Dietrich-Platz 2
T 2553 1234
www.berlin.grand.hyatt.de

Lux 11 016
Room rates:
double, from €130
Rosa-Luxemburg-Strasse 9-13
T 936 2800
www.lux-eleven.com

Mani 022
Room rates:
double, from €80;
Room 208, from €90
Torstrasse 136
T 5302 8080
www.hotel-mani.com

Michelberger Hotel 017
Room rates:
double, from €60;
Loft, from €80;
The Chalet, from €140;
The Golden One, from €140
Warschauer Strasse 39/40
T 2977 8590
www.michelbergerhotel.com

Modern Boat 016
Room rates:
boat, from €180
Gustav-Holzmann-Strasse 10
T 0176 6411 5016
www.welcomebeyond.com

WALLPAPER* CITY GUIDES

Executive Editor
Rachael Moloney

Editor
Jeremy Case

Authors
Paul Sullivan
Rachel B Doyle
Charly Wilder

Art Editor
Eriko Shimazaki
Original Design
Loran Stosskopf
Map Illustrator
Russell Bell

Photography Editor
Elisa Merlo
Assistant Photography Editor
Nabil Butt

Production Manager
Vanessa Todd-Holmes

Chief Sub-Editor
Nick Mee
Sub-Editor
Farah Shafiq

Editorial Assistant
Emilee Jane Tombs

Contributor
Sophie Lovell

Interns
Laura Hartung
Marina Hartung

Wallpaper* ® is a
registered trademark
of IPC Media Limited

First published 2007
Revised and updated
2009, 2010, 2011, 2012,
2013 and 2014

© Phaidon Press Limited

All prices are correct at
the time of going to press,
but are subject to change.

Printed in China

Phaidon Press Limited
Regent's Wharf
All Saints Street
London N1 9PA

Phaidon Press Inc
65 Bleecker Street
New York, NY 10012

Phaidon® is a registered
trademark of Phaidon
Press Limited

www.phaidon.com

A CIP Catalogue record for
this book is available from
the British Library.

ISBN 978 0 7148 6823 3

PHOTOGRAPHERS

**Bildarchiv Monheim
GmbH/Alamy**
Einsteinturm, p101

Benjamin Blossom
Hotel de Rome, pp026-027
Kosmetiksalon Babette,
pp058-059
Haus der Kulturen
der Welt, pp066-067
Olympiastadion, p089
Badeschiff, pp094-095

Bitter Bredt
GSW Headquarters, p013

Martin Brück
Bauhaus Building, p097

Roderick Coyne
Kandinsky/Klee
House, pp098-099

Michael Danner
Kaiser-Wilhelm-
Gedächtnis-Kirche, p014
Michelberger Hotel, p017
Casa Camper, p029
Reinstoff, p050
Bar Tausend, p061
Neues Museum, p069
Labels 2, pp070-071
Apartment, p084

Diephotodesigner.de
Hotel-Pension
Dittberner, pp030-031

Café Einstein, p033
Borchardt, p060
DZ Bank Building, p068

Georges Fessy
Velodrom, pp090-091

Michael Franke
Holocaust Memorial,
pp034-035
Pauly Saal, pp042-043
The Grand, p055
Philipp Schöpfer and
Daniel Klapsing, p063
Liquidrom, p092, p093

Simon Freund
Our/Berlin vodka, p083

Luca Girardini
Berlin city view,
inside front cover
Gorki Apartments, p018,
p019
25hours Hotel Bikini, p024
La Soupe Populaire, p041
Lava, p051
Glass, p054
Museum for Architectural
Drawing, p065
Galerie Ulrich Fiedler, p073
Atelier Akeef, p078
P & T, p079
Simon&Me, p082
Objets Trouvés, pp086-087

Sabine Götz
Strandbad Wannsee, p100

Frank Herfort
Mani, p022, p023
Luzia, p044, p045
Típica, p046
Lokal, p047
Andreas Murkudis,
pp074-075
Lunettes Selection, p076
Voo Store, p085

Nagib Khazaka
The Weinmeister, p025
nhow, p028
Tin, pp056-057

Noshe
ICC, p012
Sammlung Boros,
p036, p037

Peartree Digital
Lunettes Kollektion
frames, p077

Patrick Voigt
Fernsehturm, p015

**Jens Ziehe/Courtesy
the artist and Sprüth
Magers Berlin London**
Sprüth Magers, pp080-081

BERLIN
A COLOUR-CODED GUIDE TO THE HOT 'HOODS

TIERGARTEN
Many of Berlin's most remarkable buildings are in and around its central green space

SCHEUNENVIERTEL
Explore beyond the well-trodden thoroughfares to discover this area's intriguing stores

KREUZBERG
Still edgy and filled with creatives and hip eateries, this is the city's cultural melting pot

FRIEDRICHSHAIN
Communist architecture dominates the main roads while backstreets offer surprises

CHARLOTTENBURG
The capital's main retail artery is a draw, as are the upmarket restaurants and hotels

MITTE
Bomb damage has been replaced by exciting new structures in the centre of the city

PRENZLAUER BERG
This quarter is known for its 19th-century apartment blocks and weekend brunch venues

SCHÖNEBERG
Leafy boulevards and grand villas fill the old West, stretching as far as the Wannsee lakes

For a full description of each neighbourhood, see the Introduction.
Featured venues are colour-coded, according to the district in which they are located.